Abracadabra

GRAFFIX

First paperback edition 2001
First published 2001 in hardback by
A & C Black (Publishers) Ltd
37 Soho Square, London, W1D 3QZ

Text copyright © 2001 Alex Gutteridge
Illustrations copyright © 2001 Lucy Su

The rights of Alex Gutteridge and Lucy Su to be identified as
author and illustrator of this work have been asserted by them
in accordance with the Copyrights, Designs and Patents Act 1988.

ISBN 0-7136-5908-4

A CIP catalogue for this book is available from the
British Library.

Printed and bound in Spain by G. Z. Printek, Bilbao.

Abracadabra

Alex Gutteridge
Illustrated by Lucy Su

A & C Black · London

For Michael

Chapter One

I was horrified but I shouldn't have been. It was just the sort of thing Amy would do.

The whole class crowded around, waiting for my decision. Liam was sneering.

Out of the corner of my eye I saw Becca stand on tip-toe behind him and rest her chin on his shoulder. Jealousy surged through every vein in my body.

No chance. I'm not afraid of anything. Or anyone. Especially not a stupid deserted village.

How did it become deserted?

Everyone in Whittington was wiped out in the plague over 300 years ago.
The village was never inhabited again and the houses fell down and eventually became covered with grass. Just the church ruins remain.

I felt myself flushing as Becca's almond-shaped eyes fixed on my face. For once I had her attention. Amy explained.

And that's where we're going to have the disco. Whitton Farm, our house, used to be Whittington Farm.

It's O.K. The house is two fields away from the deserted village. My parents have instructions to keep their distance!

Whittington?

Becca slumped into the chair next to Liam. All the colour had drained from her face.

She shook her head and bolted for the door.

I made one last attempt to change her mind although I knew it would be hopeless.

Chapter Two

It was still and sultry on the evening of the party. I arrived early to help Amy set things up. The whole place seemed to set my nerves on edge.

It always had, ever since we were children and Amy had insisted that we played cops and robbers amongst the mounds of grass.

Uncle Matt had lent us a small generator to run the sound and disco lights from. Amy flicked a switch to test out the acoustics. Music blasted across the countryside as she danced inside the broken-down walls of the church.

She plucked a white flower from the columbine that scrambled in and out of the window arches and tucked it behind her ear.

Uncle Matt winced at the noise.

A shudder ran down my spine.

She leapt on to her dad's tractor for a lift back to the farmhouse.

I left the music on for company and lit the barbecue. Flames leapt into the balmy evening air, dispersing a cloud of thunder flies. Already the light was fading fast. We had hung jam jar lanterns among the branches of the ancient, twisted thorn trees that marked where the main street had once been.

As I lit each candle the flickering light made long shadows showing a pattern of banks and hollows.

I trod lightly, aware that parts of the buried village were only a few feet below me. I imagined falling down, down into a world of sickness and filth, of rats and huge pits filled with dead bodies. I could almost smell the bonfires, sense the panic.

A hand grabbed me on the shoulder. I jumped,
dropping the match.

Amy had changed into a long black skirt with a
strappy orange top.

She smoothed the skirt over her hips.

I wish you wouldn't do that.

What?

Creep up behind me.

I wasn't creeping. You were just miles away, that's all. Anyway, you haven't answered my question.

I didn't want to flatter my cousin too much.

It's O.K. You actually could pass for a female in that.

I'll take that as a compliment then, shall I?

I pointed across the field behind her.

Amy ran across the field to meet them.

We all laughed, and suddenly with almost everyone there I felt stupid to have made such a fuss.

Isn't this a great place to have a party?

Everyone howled in agreement.

The words almost got stuck in my throat.

She bit her bottom lip and suddenly she laughed nervously.

Have something to eat and you'll be fine.

I'll open the presents later.

I speared a sausage with a fork and offered it to Becca.

Sausage?

She shook her head and gazed around distractedly.

You were right, Tom, this place is weird. It's almost as if...

Becca ran her fingers through her dark hair, dragging it away from her face and revealing a small, coffee-coloured birthmark in her hairline.

Then she smiled.

She reached out and touched my arm.

I felt myself blush and hoped she would think that the heat from the hot coals had caused my red cheeks.

Liam came sauntering up to the barbecue and grabbed a couple of burgers.

It was as if someone had suddenly flicked a switch. She tilted her chin and pursed her lips at him.

He put his arm around her waist and I watched as they strolled away from me.

I stayed behind the barbecue turning the sausages and cooking more beefburgers until everyone had eaten.

Every time I heard Becca's laugh during a break in the music the hairs on the back of my neck rose.

My shirt was sticking to my skin. I peeled it away and sat down in front of the small copse that was over-grown with hawthorn and blackberries.

There was a rustling behind me and a whirl of cool air blew out from amongst the beech trees. I turned and rubbed my eyes.

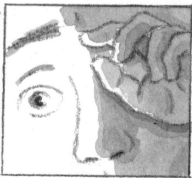

A girl stood about a metre away. Her long cream dress was almost fluorescent in the dimness and thick hair cascaded past her waist. I couldn't see her face clearly but she stood very still, like an animal trying to outwit its predator.

As I stood up and moved towards her she put her hand up to her forehead as if to shield herself. Then she spun around.

I stretched out my arm and a blackberry bramble
ripped across my skin.

The girl stopped and turned. I looked into her eyes.
For some reason she was absolutely petrified.

Chapter Four

Are you a friend of Amy's?

She didn't answer but stared straight at me, unblinking, unmoving.

I won't hurt you. My name's Tom.

I know. I've seen you here before.

She whispered so faintly I almost missed it. I craned my head to try and get a better view of her. The outline of her face looked familiar but for the moment I couldn't place it.

Becca's tinkling laugh drifted over on the night air. I turned away from the girl for a moment to see Becca lit up like a star on stage, posing in front of the disco lights.

The girl crept forwards and followed my glance.

The girl nodded and a glimmer of a smile etched the corners of her lips.

She shrugged her shoulders and stepped out of the shadows.

Her fingers were icy cold as she lifted my hand into the light from one of the candles.

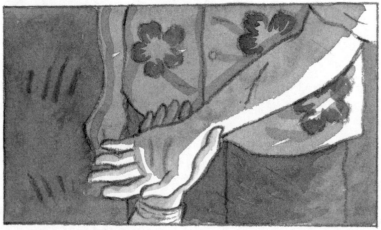

She dabbed my arm with the hem of her dress.

I began to feel odd. This girl was strange. I looked towards the others, laughing and dancing. Amy waved at me but I didn't acknowledge her. It was as if I was watching them from a long way away.

There was a churning feeling in my stomach and I felt light-headed.
Suddenly I was cold, almost shivering. My legs felt wobbly and I sat down on a mound of turf.

She crouched beside me. Her breath was sweet and spicy like cloves. It made me feel sick.

I don't understand.

I spoke quietly, not able to believe the thoughts that were crowding my brain.

Where are your parents?

She moved closer. I recoiled.

Now you are afraid of me. You are afraid to believe what your eyes are showing you and your brain is telling you. My parents are dead, wiped out in the plague.

Tears spilled down her cheeks.

I wanted to touch her but I daren't. She had seemed real enough when she had tended my arm, cold, but real flesh and blood. But now I knew that she was anything but real.

Chapter Five

Charlotte wept silently beside me. A trellis of hair covered her face.

She clutched at a triangular shaped pendant that hung around her neck. It had letters on it but I couldn't make them out.

She lifted her hair back from her face to reveal a vivid red scar at the top of her forehead.

One day they threw stones at me and I escaped into the woods but I don't blame them for what they did.

But if you had brought the disease with you, surely you would have caught it too?

This is what saved me, my good luck charm.

She tore the silver pendant from her neck.

A loud cheer rose into the sky from the disco as the music stopped abruptly and clapping thundered around the fields.

A lump rose in my throat and tears pricked behind my eyes. We sat there for what seemed like ages but must only have been a minute or so. Then she stood up.

You have been so kind.

You can't keep blaming yourself for what happened.

I hauled myself to my feet as the crowd from the disco milled towards us.

She was twisting her hair around her hand into a bun at the nape of her neck.

Suddenly the moon appeared from behind the clouds. I stared at her almond-shaped eyes, the sprinkling of freckles across her nose, the scar on her forehead and realised why she had looked familiar. I took a step backwards.

I wanted to run away but my feet were rooted to the spot.

Charlotte leant forwards and kissed me with a featherlight touch on the cheek.

She pressed something into the palm of my hand. And with a half smile she slipped back into the safety of the gloomy copse. I lifted the pendant towards the light of one of the candles and read the letters.

The demon of disease – reduced to a single letter. I'd read about that...

Chapter Six

Liam's taunt echoed into the night. A few people turned to watch before drifting homewards across the fields.

Becca tried to pull him back but Liam swaggered towards me until he was suffocatingly close.

I could feel my temples throbbing but I tried to keep my nerve. Everyone had left except for the three of us and Amy. Beads of sweat glistened on Liam's nose and around his hairline.

Becca is quite capable of speaking for herself.

I daren't look at Becca's face but every ounce of my being longed for her to come to my side and say it wasn't true.

Amy prodded Liam in the chest.

You're making a complete fool of yourself, Liam.

Her eyes blazed angrily and she gazed up at the threatening clouds.

It's going to rain.
I'd better cover the sound
equipment with some tarpaulin.

She flounced off towards the church.

You've spoiled my party.

For a moment Liam looked contrite and I let out my breath slowly. Then he spun around and grabbed my wrist. He's taller than me and strong. He took me by surprise.

He prised the pendant from the palm of my hand.

A huge crack of thunder filled the air and the ground seemed to shake underneath our feet.

Several people screamed in the distance as a flash of lightning lit up the sky and huge droplets of rain exploded on the dry earth.

Something snapped inside my head. I clenched my fist, gritted my teeth and raised my arm to hit him squarely on the jaw. I knew he'd probably pulverise me but I didn't care. I couldn't take any more and I just didn't understand what Becca saw in him.

Suddenly a strong gust of wind blasted between us, the disco lights went crazy for a few seconds and then we were immersed in darkness. Every one of the candles had blown out as the jam jars swung precariously on their branches.

I heard Becca's sharp intake of breath and I shivered as her hand clutched at mine and our fingers intertwined. As our eyes grew accustomed to the inky gloom I realised Liam hadn't moved.

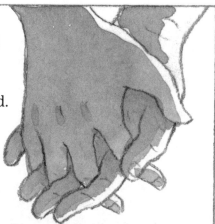

Charlotte stood next to him, appearing even more fragile than before, as if she might crumble away before our very eyes but her fingers had Liam's arm in a vice-like grip. He looked frozen with fear.

The rain stung at my face and water ran down the back of my neck. Becca leant closer.

Return the talisman.

Liam's forearm was turning white as her grip tightened.

Liam tried to loosen Charlotte's hold. But his hand plucked at his own arm as if her fingers were just an illusion and his mouth gaped open in horror.

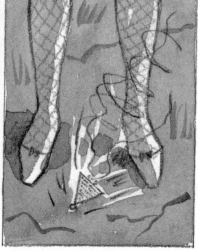

She smiled, taking a step backwards and letting go of him. Liam thrust the pendant to the ground where it spun several times before landing at Becca's feet.

I wasn't sure whether he was talking to me, Becca or
Charlotte, or all three of us, but he almost tripped
over his own feet in his hurry to get away.

I wondered if Becca would follow him but she didn't
even appear to notice he had gone. She was staring
at the pendant.

Charlotte bent down and picked it up. She held it out towards Becca.

Her voice was high-pitched now and I could feel her shaking beside me.

She looked at me pleadingly but I didn't know what to say.

Charlotte took a couple of paces forwards and placed the pendant in Becca's hand.

Becca held the triangular piece of metal gingerly as if it might burn and traced her long nails over the writing.

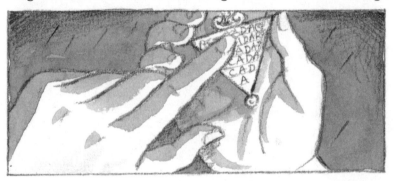

Then she looked straight into Charlotte's eyes. Even in the half-light the likeness between the two of them was unmistakable.

Becca covered her face with her hands and shook her head over and over again.

And then she fainted.

Chapter Seven

Soft, silvery moonlight filtered through the clouds
and a torch beam bounced along the church walls.

Amy! Becca's passed
out. Run and get help.
Quickly!

The rain had eased to a
soothing shower as I lifted
Becca underneath the cover
of the beech trees and
stroked the damp hair back
from her face.

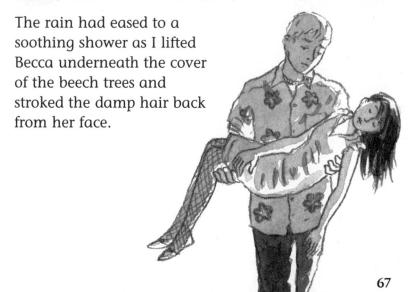

Charlotte's voice was very faint even though she crouched next to me.

I felt a knot tighten in my stomach.

Charlotte leant over and gently lifted my chin. I stared into her translucent brown eyes as if hypnotised.

Steam rose from the ground and Charlotte seemed to almost float in the mist.

I tried to catch hold of her dress as she floated away but it dissolved like cobwebs on my fingers.

Becca's eyelids flickered. For a moment she lay quite still staring into space then she turned her head towards me.

She pressed her fingers to the birthmark on her forehead.

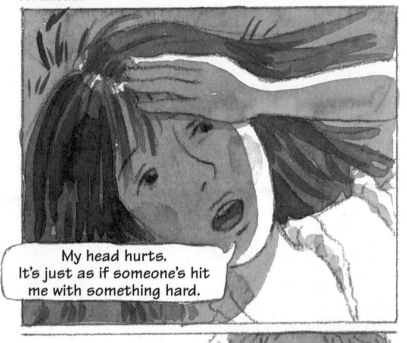

My head hurts. It's just as if someone's hit me with something hard.

You banged it when you fell. It'll be all right.

I had this awful dream about this girl who looked just like me. She'd got this scar just where my birthmark is and you know what they say...?

I tried to sound casual.

What?

That when you're reincarnated you often have marks where the dead person was injured. It seemed so real, it was almost as if she was me.

She propped herself up on her elbow and smiled.

Sounds stupid doesn't it?

I could hear the rumble of Uncle Matt's tractor approaching.

I helped Becca to her feet.

Thanks for staying with me.

She touched my arm.

Amy's always saying what a nice person you are. She's right.

I smiled as if my face was going to split in two.

The headlights from the tractor blinded us for a moment. Amy raced over and flung her arms around Becca.

Becca cast a sideways glance at me.

As Uncle Matt and Amy helped Becca to the trailor I noticed something glinting amongst the leaves on the ground. I picked it up and slipped it in my pocket.

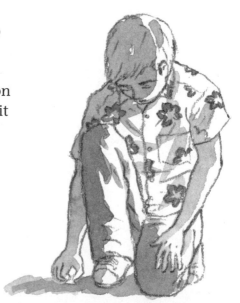

A warm wind swished at the leaves and ghostly spirals of mist danced towards the high branches. A comforting aroma of cloves filled the air.

Amy pinched my arm playfully.

So, who was that girl you were talking to? She must have been a gatecrasher.

Actually, I think we were the gatecrashers.

But the words were lost in the noise of the revving engine.

Only a couple of months to your birthday.

Another party to look forward to.

Amy chattered to Becca as we approached the farmhouse.

I rubbed the Abracadabra pendant. Soon I would give it to Becca, but not yet.

November 10th, that's your birthday isn't it, Becca?

Fancy you knowing that!

She turned and smiled at me.

We looked back towards the copse.

So, do you still think it's spooky?